10/20

GETTING TO KNOW

Apple
Swift

SHERRI MABRY GORDON

rosen publishing's
rosen
central®

New York

Published in 2019 by The Rosen Publishing Group, Inc.
29 East 21st Street, New York, NY 10010

Library of Congress Cataloging-in-Publication Data

Names: Gordon, Sherri Mabry, author.
Title: Getting to know Apple Swift / Sherri Mabry Gordon.
Description: First edition. I New York : Rosen Publishing, 2019. I Series: Code power : a teen programmer's guide I Includes bibliographical references and index. I Audience: Grades 5–8.
Identifiers: LCCN 2018007393I ISBN 9781508183648 (library bound) I ISBN 9781508183631 (pbk.)
Subjects: LCSH: Swift (Computer program language)—Juvenile literature.
Classification: LCC QA76.73.S95 G67 2019 I DDC 005.13/3—dc23
LC record available at https://lccn.loc.gov/2018007393

Manufactured in the United States of America

{ CONTENTS

$menuclass = 'horiznav';
$topmenuclass ='top menu

When Thomas Suarez was in sixth grade, he gave a TEDx Talk on the importance of technology and computer science in education. That talk has since been watched more than seven million times and has been translated into nearly forty different languages. It became one of the highest-viewed TEDx Talks of all time.

Part of the talk's allure was the fact that a sixth grader was programming apps for the iPhone, iPad, and iPod Touch and putting them in Apple's App Store. He was good at it. At the time of his TEDx talk, the twelve-year-old Suarez had already developed two successful apps. The first app was called Earth Fortune, which was a unique fortune-teller app that would display different colors of the earth depending on what the user's fortune was. While this app was successful, the app that got him the most attention was his Bustin Jieber app. This app was a lot like whack-a-mole—except instead of a mole, users would whack pop star Justin Bieber.

"I created [Bustin Jieber] because a lot of people at school disliked Justin Bieber a little bit. So, I decided to make the app," Suarez explains in his TEDx Talk. "A lot of kids these days

>> Young coder Thomas Suarez's TEDx Talk on the importance of technology has been viewed more than seven million times.

like to play games [but] not many kids know where to go to find out how to make a program."

Apple's release of the iPhone with the iPhone software development kit (SDK) opened a whole new world of possibilities for Suarez and kids like him. At the time, the SDK, which was a suite of tools for creating and programming in iPhone apps, required him to use the Objective-C programming language because Swift did not yet exist. Even then, Suarez was able to demonstrate that a person does not have to be an adult, own a big company, have a lot of money, or even have a degree in computer science to learn how to program. All anyone needs is an idea and the time and determination to see it through.

"Bustin Jieber and Suarez prove that app development, coding and design are, on the whole, becoming increasingly accessible both to young people and those without computer science graduate degrees," writes Rip Empson of TechCrunch. "Even if his apps aren't gold-caliber, he's 12 years old. We talk a lot about the U.S. 'no longer making anything,' but if more kids like Thomas take up the reins, the U.S. and the world at large will no doubt be better off."

Even better for kids today is that programming an app for the iPhone is even easier than it was when Suarez first started making apps. Today, Apple offers a unique programming language called Swift that is not only user-friendly but also fun to use. It has many interesting features, and it is easy for anyone to download the tools needed—Xcode, the SDK, and Swift Playgrounds—and get started.

CHAPTER 1

A SWIFT BEGINNING: HOW IT ALL STARTED

I t is hard to imagine a life without technology. After all, people use it every day. To wake up in the morning, someone might use the alarm clock function on their iPhone. Then they might do their homework on a computer, message their friends, and play their favorite online games. People also shop online, download books onto a tablet, and watch Netflix on their laptops.

Without these advances in technology, modern life would not be as easy or as convenient. These technologies do not create themselves. A development team programs all these pieces of technology. These teams are made up of computer programmers who put a lot of time and energy into writing code so that technology performs the way it is expected to.

HOW IT ALL WORKS

Every piece of technology speaks its own language. This language is called code. For instance, code tells an Apple Watch to keep

>> Wearable technology, such as this Apple Watch, requires good code to function properly. Code is how a seemingly simple watch can remind its wearer to remain physically active.

track of wearers' steps or remind them to stand every hour. Code also tells an iPhone to play certain ringtones based on who is calling or remind people a second time when they have not read a text message. It even powers all the games and apps that get stored on an iPhone.

There are countless other ways code is used every day to make technology work, and there are hundreds of different coding languages in the programming world that help get the job done. In fact, every language has a different name. Some popular languages include Java, C/C++, Ruby, Python, JavaScript, and Objective-C.

Among the newest, and the easiest to learn, is the programming language Swift. Developed in 2014 by Apple, Swift was released not only to work alongside Apple's existing programming language, Objective-C, but also to eventually replace it. Apple wanted to create a programming language that was not only easy to use but also saved developers a lot of time and energy.

HOW IT ALL BEGAN

Chris Lattner, a former Apple executive, is the man behind the creation of Swift. Lattner, who joined Apple in 2005, spent a year and a half creating this new programming language, and he never mentioned it to anyone—not even his closest friends. Working mostly at night and on weekends, Lattner started creating Swift in 2010. Within a year, he had mapped out the basics of the new language and was ready to reveal his secret project to the top executives at Apple. They were so impressed with Lattner's work that they put a few other engineers on the project to help him.

>> Swift was developed by Chris Lattner, who spent a year and a half creating the programming language without ever telling anyone he was working on it.

After about eighteen months of work on the project, developing Swift became a major focus for Apple. By this time, Apple had assigned a huge team to work alongside Lattner. Together, they created a faster and more effective way to build software apps for iPhones, iPads, and Macs. Now, it can even be used for Apple Watch and Apple TV.

On an episode of *Accidental Tech* podcast, Lattner said:

Initially, it was really just me messing around and nobody knew about it because there wasn't anything to know about. But eventually, it got a little more serious … So I started talking to my management and some of the engineers that were working on Clang [another project I was working on] and they seemed excited about it. [Eventually] I convinced my manager that it was interesting enough that we should have a couple of people work on it.

When Apple debuted Swift in 2014 at its Worldwide Developer Conference (WWDC), the world was shocked. No one had any idea this project was even in the works. It was an instant hit. In fact, by January 2018, just four years after being released, Swift was ranked twelfth out of hundreds of languages by the Tiobe Index, which specializes in tracking software. Meanwhile, Objective-C, the language that Swift was designed to replace, was ranked sixteenth.

This high ranking is a pretty big deal for such a new programming language. Typically, when a new programming language appears out of nowhere, it takes some time before a lot of people start using it. For instance, Google unveiled a language called Go in 2009, five years before Swift was unveiled, and the Tiobe Index ranks it lower than Swift.

Part of the reason Swift is so popular is because it is so easy and fun to use. In addition, it is built so that anyone can learn how to code using Swift—even someone who has never programmed anything before. Another reason why Swift is catching on so fast is that hundreds of thousands of developers build apps for iPhones, iPads, Apple Watches, and Macs on a daily basis. With

>> Apple debuted Swift in 2014 at the WWDC. Since then, it has been warmly received around the globe.

so many of these devices in the marketplace, it is not surprising that Swift already has a mass following.

Lattner wrote on his personal home page:

I [hoped] that by making programming more approachable and fun, we'll appeal to the next generation of programmers and to help redefine how computer science is taught. The aim is not only to make coding easier, but to provide a better way of learning to program—to bring this skill to a whole new type of person.

>>THE MAN BEHIND APPLE SWIFT

Chris Lattner is a software developer who has created a number of important technology projects. In addition to his contribution to Swift, he also created the Clang compiler as well as designed the LLVM compiler optimization infrastructure. A compiler is a program that converts instructions into a form that can be read and executed by a computer. When it comes to Clang and LLVM, Clang works on the front end of the project, and LLVM works on the back end. Typically, the front end means the parts of the project that the user will interact with. Meanwhile, the back end means the parts that do the work that the user cannot see.

After developing Swift, Lattner left Apple. In August 2017, he went to work for Google Brain. Google Brain is part of Google's focus on deep learning and artificial intelligence. Deep learning is a machine learning technique whereby a machine learns tasks directly from data. Meanwhile, artificial intelligence is the ability of computer systems to perform tasks that normally require human intelligence, such as speech recognition, decision making, and visual perception.

Since Lattner joined Google, there have been talks that the company may include some of Swift's elements in a new operating system (OS) it is developing. Although these speculations started out as mere rumors, tech experts wonder if Lattner's presence at Google could bridge the gap between Apple and Google.

WHY APPLE CREATED SWIFT

Apple has a philosophy that everyone should have "the opportunity to create something that can change the world." Because of that, it wanted to create a programming language that allowed the average person to build apps that bring his or her ideas to life.

As a result, it designed Swift to be straightforward and easy to use. The idea is that even if a person has never coded anything before, it will be simple to learn how to code using the Swift programming language. One way the developers accomplished this goal was by providing an environment where users can see if what they are doing is working the way they want it to.

For example, when people program with Swift, they are able to see what they are creating and developing right in front of them while they are writing it. Users can type their code on the left and immediately see the result on the right. Plus, Apple designed Swift to use words that most people already know, such as "print," "add," and "remove." This eliminates the need to learn a lot of complicated coding terms.

A CLOSER LOOK AT SWIFT

When beginners are learning to code, they are learning how to solve problems in creative ways. Swift allows users the opportunity to be imaginative in an environment that this easy to master. Overall, it is a general-purpose programming language that is not only powerful but enjoyable to use.

Before Swift was created, apps for the iPhone and other Apple products were programmed using Objective-C. Objective-C is a programming language that was created in the 1980s and was based on the popular programming language C. However, Objective-C was not as easy to use as more modern programming languages, such as Python and Ruby. That has all changed since Swift has been implemented. Now, developers who create apps for Apple products are flocking to Swift because it is a more modern programming language that makes programming simple, fun, and fast.

"Swift is a big advance over Objective-C," said Jeff Bailey in an interview. Bailey is an iOS developer and principal at FourthFrame Technologies, a consulting company located in Columbus, Ohio. "Objective-C can do a lot of things, but it also has a lot of sharp edges. Meanwhile, Swift is a safe, fun, easy-to-use modern language. For people who are familiar with more modern languages it offers a natural transition."

Overall, Apple's goal with Swift was to make writing and maintaining programs easier for the developer. As a result, Apple designed the language with the following characteristics in mind:

- **Swift is safe**. Apple believes that anytime a developer writes code, it should behave in a safe manner. In other words, developer mistakes should be caught before the software is in production. To some developers, Swift may feel strict at times, but Apple says that strictness will save developers time in the long run. Mistakes are caught ahead of time, and there is no need for a lot of corrections down the road.
- **Swift is fast**. According to Apple, one goal with Swift is to replace languages like Objective-C, which was used for developing software for Apple devices in the past. The C-based languages are typically known for

being fast, and Swift is right on par with their speed. Additionally, it is as predictable and consistent as it is fast, making it the best of both worlds.

- **Swift is expressive**. Designed with all the modern features that developers love and expect in a new language, Swift is constantly evolving and keeping pace with the demands and changes of the programming world. As a result, Apple monitors and embraces language advancements that work and implements them into its updates.

>> Swift was designed to replace Objective-C, which is a complex programming language that can sometimes be hard to use.

Other features in Swift include its ability to infer types, eliminate headers, provide namespaces, and manage memory automatically. Swift does not even use semicolons, which are common in most programming languages.

"Together all the features of Swift create a programming language that is powerful and yet fun to use," said Bailey. "It allows you to express your ideas in a more natural way, to be more productive and to create less bugs than you might in Objective-C."

CHAPTER 2

JUST HOW SWIFT IS IT? WHAT REAL USERS THINK

W hether a person enjoys running or just hitting the gym, the trend in exercise is to focus on interval training. Unfortunately for many exercise enthusiasts, keeping track of the work they are doing in the gym is not always easy. To meet this need, Jeff Bailey created the app Intervals.

Intervals allows users to customize their interval and circuit training. It also features various audio settings, warm-up and cooldown options, and a variety of different workouts. The app also allows users to add their own workouts or use the preloaded workouts and change them to make them their own.

"It is the perfect app for the person who wants to go from the couch to a 5K," Bailey explained.

When Bailey began working on his popular app in 2014, Apple Swift had not yet been released. As a result, the programming that he did for the app was all done in Objective-C. So naturally,

>> The app Intervals, designed using Swift and Objective-C by iOS developer Jeff Bailey, allows users to customize their interval training. It is just one example of Swift's flexibility.

when Swift came out, he was a little hesitant after all the work he had put into his project. Yet, because Swift had such a passionate following almost from day one, he was interested in learning more about it.

What he discovered was that Swift is a very accessible and easy-to-use language that can cut down on the time spent coding. Plus, he was able to gradually update his Intervals app using Swift. While there are still some parts that are programmed using Objective-C, a lot of it is now programmed in Swift.

"The two languages work really well together, which makes it easy for developers to add Swift features gradually into existing projects," Bailey said.

REAL SWIFT

Overall, developers such as Bailey approve of Swift. In fact, when Swift was introduced at the WWDC, the audience of developers roared with appreciation for the new programming language. Finally, there would be an easier way to develop apps for Apple products. Plus, Swift borrowed the best elements from popular and more modern programming languages, such as Python and JavaScript, which made it even more attractive. Just a year after it was released, it became the "most loved" technology, according to the 2015 Stack Overflow Developer Survey. Swift was also listed among the top ten "most wanted" technologies.

Bailey said:

Swift is a great programming language. I have really enjoyed learning it. What's more, it was a good move on Apple's part. Objective-C was getting a little old and a lot of new languages were coming on the scene. Swift is much more modern and approachable. It is type-safe and allows you to express your ideas in a seamless way.

The other big idea behind Swift that really appeals to programmers is that fact that they can write their code and see the results in real time. Under the old model for coding, developers write lines and lines of code in a text box and then compile those results. That process can sometimes take a long time before they see the end result. With Swift, developers can tweak their code and watch the changes happen right in the same coding environment. What this means for developers is that they can play around with concepts faster and create projects more quickly.

Most developers agree that Swift creates a much nicer learning environment. Not only is the code easier to learn, but being able to see what you are creating while you are writing it has a lot of benefits. Most agree the ease of using Swift will attract a bigger pool of developers focused on Apple products, especially as young coders start learning the language.

>>SWIFT OVER C

Not only is Swift easier to use than Objective-C, it is also easier to learn. Plus, developers can do a lot more with a lot less in Swift, which is why it is a better choice for a lot of software. Here are some advantages Swift has over Objective-C:

- Swift is easier to read because it closely resembles the English language.
- Swift is a safer programming language and has built-in error handling tools that Objective-C does not have.
- Swift requires less code to get things done, so you can write a program much faster.
- Swift operates much faster than Objective-C and is close to the same speed as the C++ programming language.
- Swift is easier to maintain over time even as it grows in size and complexity.

BENEFITS OF LEARNING SWIFT

For developers who are already experts in Objective-C, switching to Swift might be a tough sell, especially if they are already productive while using it and their apps are performing well. For beginner coders, however, the benefits of using Swift are more compelling. It is much easier and faster to get started developing apps with Swift than it would be if a person tried to learn Objective-C. Here are just a few of the other top reasons why beginners should learn to program using Swift:

- **Swift is easy to learn**. Apple designed Swift to be easy to learn. What this means is that anyone can begin building apps much faster than he or she would be able to on any other development platform. In fact, some experts say that it may only take a couple of months for someone to build an app from start to finish.
- **Swift is an approachable language**. Typically, when people are learning to code, they have to learn new coding languages. With Swift, users can learn as they go. Because they can see what is happening in their app as they go along, they will learn the concepts behind Swift very quickly.
- **Swift is the future of Apple development**. Because so many people around the globe use Apple devices, it makes sense to learn the programming language that the company prefers. Since the launch of the App Store, Apple says it has handed over billions of dollars to developers in the United States alone. Judging by the success of the company, it makes sense to support

iOS, macOS, watchOS, tvOS, and any future platforms it creates.

- **Swift allows users to experiment**. With Swift Playgrounds—an app anyone can download on the iPad, as well as the "playground" mode inside of Xcode, the development environment used to write Swift code—users can discover new ideas for their apps. There are lots of templates, puzzles, and scenarios to play around with. Because this work is separate from the app project itself, users can see what works and what does not work without impacting their overall app.

>> Swift Playgrounds is an app anyone can download and use without much training. Playgrounds is also available inside of Xcode.

- **Swift is a good starting point**. Apple worked really hard to make sure that it is easy to learn Swift. The development team used elements from other languages that work well and got rid of the things that did not work well. As a result, once someone learns how to program using Swift, other programming languages might look familiar or make more sense. If users have programmed before using a different language, they will see that Swift's syntax and concepts resemble some of the ones they already use. (Syntax refers to the set of rules, principles, and processes that are part of the structure of a programming language.)
- **Swift programming is in demand**. Lots of companies in the job market want to build apps and programs for Apple devices. That means if someone knows how to program using Swift, there is a good chance it will not be hard to find a job in which skills developing for iOS, macOS, watchOS, and more are needed.

Overall, Swift is the direction most developers are taking when it comes to developing for Apple devices. Many would agree that Objective-C is starting to look outdated and will eventually become a less popular programming language.

Until that happens, the two programming languages will continue to coexist. The good news is that Swift is perfectly compatible with Objective-C, and they can be used interchangeably within the same project, just like Bailey did with his Intervals app. This feature is especially useful when projects are being extended or updated.

CHAPTER 3

SWIFT 101: GETTING STARTED CODING

Coding, or computer programming, is the art of using a programming language like Swift to instruct a computer to perform certain functions. While this may sound extremely challenging, it can also be a lot of fun. Not only do users get to solve puzzles and impress people with their creations, but they also feel a sense of pride when they learn how to create something that can control what a device does.

THE BASICS OF PROGRAMMING

When creating apps, whether using Swift or another coding language, it helps to know how everything works. First, an app is a set of written instructions for a computer to follow. In other words, an app performs a task for the user. For instance, a phone's weather app predicts the local weather, while the games on a phone provide users with hours of entertainment. Apps like these, which are run on a cell phone or tablet, are sometimes called mobile apps. They have a lot in common with the apps that run on a computer.

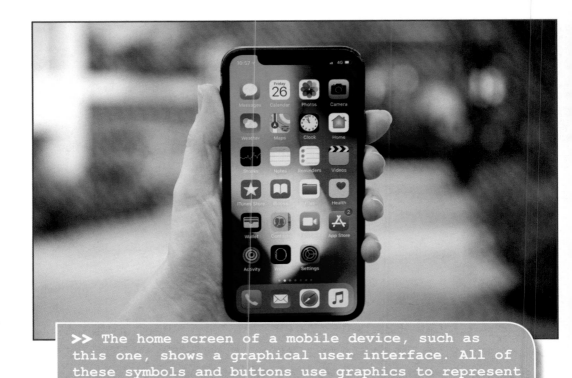

>> The home screen of a mobile device, such as this one, shows a graphical user interface. All of these symbols and buttons use graphics to represent what their application is.

When opening an app on an iPhone or on a Mac, typically a graphical user interface (GUI) appears. A GUI might consist of pictures, text boxes, buttons, or other graphics. Behind each of these elements are lines of code, sometimes called instructions. This code tells the computer what steps to take, depending on what the user does. As a result, every time users push a button or click on a picture in an app, the code is behind the scenes telling the computer what to do. Sometimes code is simple, and sometimes it is complicated, but no program will work unless there is code telling it what to do.

GETTING STARTED

To code using Swift, users will need an Apple device, such as a Mac computer. Ideally, the Mac will be running macOS 10.12.6 or higher. If a Swift learner does not know which version of macOS he or she is running, it is possible to click on the Apple icon in the upper left-hand corner and select About This Mac. If the Mac does not have macOS 10.12.6 or higher, then it may be necessary to do a software update to start coding with Swift.

Once users have the right version of macOS, they also will need to download Xcode and the iOS software development kit (SDK). Xcode is a code editor that was developed by Apple. It not only lets users write code, but it also includes a simulator. The simulator allows users to see how their code will run on any type of Apple device. Meanwhile, the SDK is a collection of prebuilt programming libraries that help users write apps quickly. The libraries included are collections of software that can be used when programming.

To install Xcode on a Mac, users must go to the App Store and search for Xcode. From there, they simply download and install Xcode. It is free and comes with the SDK, so everything is installed with a few clicks. Once Xcode is installed, users can open the program and click on "Create a New Xcode Project." Each time a new project is started, users will need to decide whether they want to create something for iOS, watchOS, tvOS, macOS, or cross-platform. They also will need to decide what kind of app they want to make before they begin.

CODING THE HELLO WORLD APP

For this exercise, you will need to click iOS in the upper left-hand corner and select Single View App. Xcode will then ask you to set a few options for your new app. In the section marked Product Name, give your app the name Hello World. Next, click on Add Account. Doing so will prompt you to sign in with your Apple ID. Once you have signed in, you should see your Apple account listed, and you can close the window.

Next, you will need to add an organization name and set the language option to Swift. For the organization name, there are several options: make up a company name, use your real name, or choose something else entirely. Once that is completed, click Next and then click Create. Once you click Create, your new application will be saved, and the program will launch Xcode. Your new Hello World Xcode project will open.

On the left side of your Xcode window, you will see a pane. This pane contains the files and folders that make up your project. You should select Main Storyboard from this list. This will give you a picture-book view of the device screens when you run your app. You also can use the storyboard to design all the screens and the connections between them. Although you do not have to use the storyboard when you are building an app, many find that it is much easier to do it this way. The other option is to write all of your app's design elements in code.

On the right side of your Xcode window, you will see another pane. This pane contains different tools that you can use. It is often called the Utilities Pane. Inside the Utilities Pane, toward the bottom of the screen, there is a circle inside of a box. By

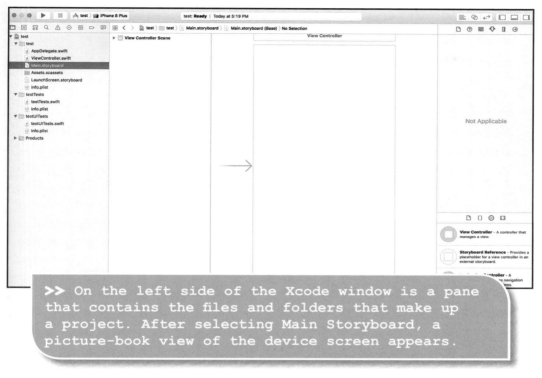

>> On the left side of the Xcode window is a pane that contains the files and folders that make up a project. After selecting Main Storyboard, a picture-book view of the device screen appears.

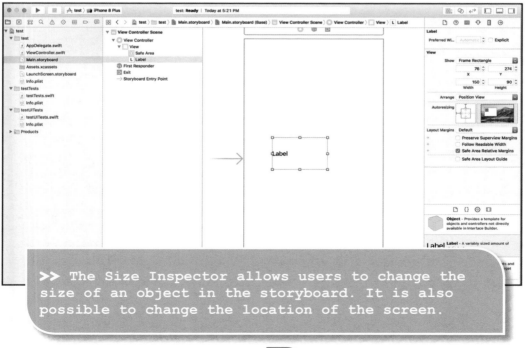

>> The Size Inspector allows users to change the size of an object in the storyboard. It is also possible to change the location of the screen.

clicking on this icon, you will be able to scroll up and down the Object Library. Scroll until you find the word Label. Next, you will want to select it and drag it into the View Controller Section.

Once the Label has been placed in the View Controller Section, you should click on the symbol in the Utilities Pane that looks like a ruler. This is called the Size Inspector. The Size Inspector allows you to change the size of an object in the storyboard. To make the label bigger, change the width and height in the Size Inspector. It is also possible to change the location on the screen. Simply specify what you want the X and Y coordinates to be. The X variable refers to the horizontal position of the element, while the Y variable refers to the vertical position.

Although you can choose any size you want and any coordinates you want, for this exercise, put 200 in the width box and 40 in the height box of the Size Inspector. Then, put 80 in the box marked X and 40 in the box marked Y. These numbers will tell Xcode how big you want the type to be and where you want it located. Now, you can move on to change the text of the Label. To do this, switch to the Attributes Inspector, which is the icon to the left of the ruler. Once there, enter Hello World into the Label text field.

Next, you can change the font if you want. Click the T icon in the Font field and then change the font style to Bold and the font size to 30. You also can change the alignment of the text by clicking on the icon that represents "centering the type" in the Alignment field. Once that step is completed, it is time to test the new app.

Try running the app and see what happens. To do this, click the Play button in the upper left-hand corner of Xcode or choose the menu option Product and then select Run. Be patient if it takes a little time for the simulator to turn itself on and load. You just programmed your first app. If you want to stop the app, click the square in the upper left-hand corner of Xcode or go to Product and then select Stop in the menu.

SWIFT ON THE PLAYGROUND

Even after creating an app using Xcode, getting familiar with Swift might take some time, especially when it comes time to write actual code. One easy way to get familiar with the programming language is to play around a little first and see what Swift is like and what it can do. In fact, one of Swift's most interesting features is its interactive environment called a Playground.

One of the best options for experimenting is by downloading Swift Playgrounds on an iPad. This app makes learning Swift interactive and fun by providing puzzles to solve. As users solve the puzzles, they learn to master Swift. In addition, using Swift Playgrounds on the iPad does not require any coding knowledge. So, it is perfect for anyone who is just learning to code. If someone does not have an iPad, Xcode also comes with a type of Playgrounds as well. In fact, Playgrounds was first introduced in Xcode as a way to experiment with code that is being written.

To get to a Playground in Xcode, users launch Xcode and go to the Welcome screen. On the Welcome screen, there is an option called Get Started with a Playground. After selecting that option, the next step is to answer a number of other questions, including what users want to name this project and whether they want to use it for iOS or macOS. Then, a number of templates

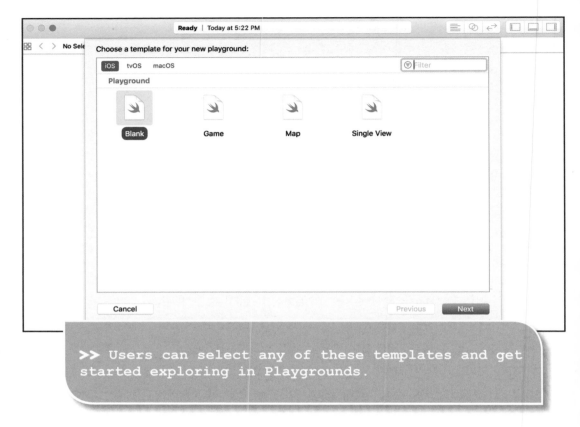

to choose from should appear. Users can select any of them and get started playing.

With Playgrounds, as users write code on one side of the screen, they can see the results appear on the other side. In other words, with Playgrounds inside of Xcode, they can watch their program run while they are writing it. Basically, the tool allows users to add new code or to change code while the software is running. This feature makes it easier and faster for people to learn how to program with Swift. The instant feedback provided by Playgrounds can be instrumental in getting beginners interested in coding.

Jeff Bailey agrees that the Swift Playgrounds app is a great tool for beginners just getting started with Swift. "It is an excellent way to learn," he said. "Even just playing around with coding in general is a great way to learn. With Swift, it is easy to try something new and get immediate feedback to see if it works. It's also a fun way to get introduced to Swift."

MOVING ON TO BIGGER AND BETTER APPS

After completing the Hello World app and experimenting with Playgrounds, it is time to start doing more complicated things. To get started coding, people need an idea. For instance, do they want to create an app that helps them keep track of their homework assignments? Or maybe they would like to create a game inspired by the Olympics? Whatever the idea, it helps to put it down on paper and to make a plan. Here are some tips for putting together a plan.

Define the project. What is the app supposed to do? Think about how users will interact with it and what functions the app should perform. Then write down all the goals. Try to think of as many scenarios as possible so that it will be easier to anticipate what might need to be done once coding begins.

Write a plan. Without a plan, even the best coders do not have any direction on what to do first. As a result, it is important to think about what type of code will be used to make the plan work. Sketch it out in as much detail as possible. Once there is a rough idea of where the app is going, it is time to get to work. Sit down and get started.

>>LYFT, THANKS TO SWIFT

Swift is a clean programming language, and it often requires less Swift code than, for example, Objective-C code, to accomplish the same task. One example of Swift's efficiency

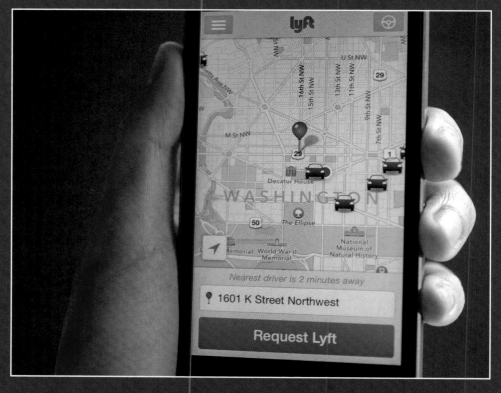

>> One example of Swift's efficiency can be seen in the redesign of the Lyft app. The older, non-Swift version of the app contained about three times as much coding.

can be seen in a case study of the Lyft app. Lyft is a ride-sharing program that people use, similar to calling a taxi or using the similar Uber app.

Once Swift came out, the company decided to rewrite its entire iOS app using Swift. What it discovered is that its old codebase had about seventy-five thousand lines of code—but the new Swift version had about twenty-five thousand lines of code. Even with much less code, the app was able to do all the things that the older version could do. Lyft also added a new onboarding process when rewriting the app. An onboarding process refers to the application process that drivers go through to work with Lyft. Engineers discovered that developing the old onboarding process took multiple people more than a month to accomplish, but the new onboarding process took one engineer less than a week to complete.

Some other companies that have used Swift to develop their applications include Khan Academy, LinkedIn, Coursera, Pandora, Vimeo, Twitter, Fitbit, and Groupon.

Accept that changes might be necessary. Once the app starts coming together, it is completely fine to make changes. It is possible to find that things are not working exactly as expected. Or, it is possible to discover a better way to do something. The trick is to be flexible and open to making changes as needed. The best programmers are those who are flexible and willing to try new things.

WHAT'S SO SNAPPY ABOUT SWIFT?

According to Bailey, Swift is a great first programming language. Plus, once you learn Swift, it will be a lot easier to learn other languages. For instance, some other programming languages are similar in syntax to Swift. Apple tried to incorporate some of the best practices from other languages into Swift.

"What's more, many popular programming languages can trace their heritage back to C," Bailey said. "If you learn Swift, you may find it is easier to learn other programming languages as well."

>> Learning to program can help teach how things work. People who understand programming can use their skills to get much more out of devices they use every day.

Even for those with no intention of ever becoming a computer programmer, learning a programming language like Swift is a great skill to have. Not only will it enhance your creativity, it will help you become a better problem solver. Additionally, if you regularly use a computer or a mobile device, then learning to program helps you understand how things work. Your skills can be used to improve the technology if you want. For instance, if you see issues or needs as you use your devices, then you also will have the ability to address them by creating something that makes life easier or more convenient.

"Even if you don't think you want to develop software in the future, you still need to know the basics of how a computer works and how programs work," Bailey explained. "Besides that, a lot of teens have iOS devices. How cool is it to build an app that will run on something you have in your pocket?"

CHAPTER 4

MOVING SWIFTLY: AN OVERVIEW OF SWIFT'S FUTURE

Ever since the first iPhone debuted in 2007, the world has widely adopted these pocket-sized computers with touchscreens. In fact, Apple announced in 2016 that the total number of active Apple devices has surpassed one billion. That is a lot of reasons to learn how to program for these popular devices using Swift.

"Everyone is learning Swift, it seems," said Jim Power, executive director of technology for Duet Health, located in central Ohio. "For the most part, developers are moving to Swift because it is safer, more concise and more fun to write."

In addition, the options for using Swift have expanded somewhat since it was first introduced. In the beginning, Swift could only be used for developing apps for the iPhone, iPad, and Mac. It has since expanded to include the Apple Watch and Apple TV. Experts believe that there is even some movement toward using Swift on the server side of development, especially with Linux.

>> Experts believe that in the future, Swift will be usable on the server side of development, especially with Linux, whose penguin mascot is world famous.

"Because Swift is now open-sourced, the language can be expanded to other platforms beyond just what Apple has created," said Power. "For example, you now can use Swift on Linux … this is really exciting for developers who want to write code server-side."

THE FUTURE IS BRIGHT

Another potential area where Swift may flourish is in the development of web applications. If Swift is being used on Linux, that means that Swift apps could run on low-cost, low-maintenance Linux servers. In fact, there are already frameworks for Swift that make it possible for Linux-based server apps to be built within Xcode. This would enable businesses to hire Swift developers to build the APIs and services they need. (An API, short for "application program interface," specifies how different software components should interact and is often used when programming GUI components.)

"There is already support for Linux," said Power. "There were even some rumors that Google might experiment with Swift in Android development." Android is a popular, Linux-based mobile phone OS developed by Google. In addition to powering smartphones, it also powers watches, tablets, and even car stereos.

As soon as Apple released Swift to the open-source community, IBM came up with a way to code with Swift in the cloud, with IBM Swift Sandbox. The cloud refers to a service that makes computer software and hardware available to anyone over the internet.

While users are not able to create a large Swift program in Sandbox, it is possible to familiarize oneself with the new programming language, which is very useful for students in the classroom setting. Additionally, because IBM and Apple have such a strong partnership, many tech experts feel that IBM will highlight more Swift implementations in the future. In doing so, it will help Swift become the go-to language for app development.

>> IBM and Apple have a strong partnership. As a result, industry experts believe IBM will highlight more uses of Swift in the future, making it even more popular for programming apps.

SWIFTLY BRIDGING THE GAP?

Some experts, including Power, believe that because Swift is now open source—meaning that the code is open or available to anyone—there is a chance that Google may adopt some of Swift's elements.

In fact, tech experts report that Google is developing a new OS called Fuchsia. Although there is very little information available indicating how Fuchsia will be used, some reporters have been told "it could potentially run computers as well as smartphones."

>>APPLE DEVELOPER ACADEMY

Apple has built an elite school in Naples, Italy, for people interested in learning how to become developers. One principle of the educational atmosphere in this school is the concept of challenge-based learning.

According to Apple, challenge-based learning teaches students to leverage technology to solve complex, real-world problems. This style of teaching pushes students to find their own answers to problems. As a result, students in the academy are not given a list of instructions on how to build an app. Instead, they are told to develop the best software they can. What the instructors hope will happen is that students will not only learn but also discover how to find the information they need.

Students are accepted into the program after taking an entrance exam. When making a decision on whom to accept, Apple is not always looking for seasoned programmers. It is more interested in how well potential applicants solve problems. As a result, the exam does not include many coding questions but instead contains questions that require logic, comprehension, and critical thinking.

While at the school, students are learning to create apps using Swift. Professors at the school argue that students spend a lot of time learning things that will be just as relevant if the students come to develop Android apps or some other kind of product entirely. Large chunks of the curriculum are focused on things like marketing, design, communication, and teamwork. In the end, the academy is hoping to turn out entrepreneurial developers who use whatever language they choose.

"What we think is known is that [Fuchsia] will carry a little bit of Apple's Open Source Swift in its tank," wrote Jonny Evans in *Computerworld*. "I'm guessing that's got something to do with [the fact that] leading Swift creator ... Chris Lattner ... now works at Google."

While this rumor does not mean that Google is basing the new OS on Swift alone, this move is in line with Apple's goal of having Swift used across many different devices, not just its own. It could mean good things for anyone who knows how

>> If Google decides to incorporate Swift into its new OS, Apple will be another step closer to achieving its goal of having Swift used on many different devices—not just Apple products.

to program using Swift. Not only could apps created for iOS devices be released more quickly for Google's OS, it also would mean more demand for Swift developers. Still, there is no way of knowing for sure if this will happen.

"It may all turn out to be meaningless," Evans wrote. "Google has a track record of creating solutions it then cancels, so it is possible this new OS will never see the light of day." Still, the thought of the two giants working together has the tech community excited.

THE DEMAND FOR SWIFT PROGRAMMERS IS SKYROCKETING

Countless studies have shown that the interest in Swift and the demand for Swift programmers is growing quickly. According to Toptal, a freelance developer placement firm, the year-to-year growth in job requests for Swift projects rose 600 percent in 2015. That is roughly triple the rate of many other languages.

Some would argue that this high growth is to be expected. After all, it is a new programming language that is used primarily for the widely popular iPhone and other Apple devices. On GitHub, a web-based hosting service, references to Swift have shown that it is experiencing unprecedented growth as well. The time to start learning Swift is now.

In addition, Power has argued that students do not need to wait until they graduate from college to start earning money programming with Swift. Aside from the money they can make from developing apps on their own time, there also are companies out there willing to pay them to program regardless of their

>> Though Swift is growing in popularity, Java is still the most popular programming language in the world. Surveys have shown that huge numbers of developers prefer Java for coding.

education level. As long as someone is proficient in Swift, he or she can start making money programming.

In fact, Power regularly hires student interns who have experience programming with Swift. They are hired to work on development teams with more experienced developers and are paid as much as twenty-two dollars an hour for their services. This is a pretty good part-time job for a student and can go a long way in helping them build a solid portfolio.

Still, it is important to point out that even though Swift is becoming increasingly popular, it is still not the most popular language for building apps. According to one survey conducted by the mobile ad network InMobi, Java is still the most popular. In fact, the survey shows that of the 1,085 mobile app developers InMobi spoke with, 65 percent preferred Java. Still, nearly 20 percent of app developers reported using Swift. According to InMobi, this is a fairly large share of the programming pie, given the fact that the language has only been around since 2014. These types of numbers show not only how much potential Swift has to change programming for the better, but also why it might be beneficial for beginners to start learning how to program with it.

>>COMPUTER PROGRAMMING AND THE JOB MARKET

According to Code.org, an organization dedicated to increasing school participation in computer science education, "Every child should have a chance to learn about algorithms, how to make an app or how the Internet works just like they learn about photosynthesis, the digestive system or electricity." Unfortunately, only 40 percent of schools teach computer programming, and only fourteen states have created computer science standards. Yet the demand for computer programming is staggeringly high. For instance:

- Computing jobs are the number one source of new wages in the United States, and there are about half a million current job openings in every industry and in every state. Additionally, these jobs are projected to grow at twice the rate of all other jobs.
- Of all the new jobs in science, technology, engineering, and math (STEM), 58 percent of those jobs are in computing. However, only 8 percent of STEM graduates have degrees in computer science.
- Young women who take advanced placement (AP) computer science in high school are ten times more likely to major in it in college. Additionally, black and Hispanic students who take AP computer science are seven times more likely to pursue a computer science degree in college.
- A computer science major can earn 40 percent more than the average college graduate. In fact, the lifetime earnings for a computer science major average $1.67 million.
- The Bureau of Labor Statistics predicts that software developer jobs will grow 17 percent between 2014 and 2024. This is much faster than the average rate of other professions. Application developer jobs alone, like those that require knowledge of Swift, are projected to grow 19 percent during that time frame.
- The US Department of Labor projects that by 2020, universities in the United States will be able to fill less than one-third of the 1.4 million computer-related job openings.

NO TIME LIKE THE PRESENT

If you are interested in developing apps for the iPhone, iPad, or Apple Watch, or if you have interest in developing software for the Mac, there is no better time than now to learn Swift. Not only will Swift eventually edge out Objective-C, but some say it may even replace C for embedded programs on Apple platforms.

"Swift has the potential to become the de-facto programming language for creating immersive, responsive, consumer-facing applications for years to come," tech expert Paul Solt wrote in *InfoWorld*. "[Part of this has to do with the fact that] Apple's intent was to make app development easier and more approachable than with any other development tool chain."

>> Apple's logo is one of the most recognizable brands in history; with the full weight of the company behind Swift, there is no doubt it will continue to grow in popularity and usefulness.

In addition, Swift was not built just to support Apple's product goals. It was built with the future in mind. It takes what is great about other languages and combines that with some new language features that make it really fresh and exciting to use. The possibilities for future uses are endless, especially with two of the industry's biggest companies— Apple and IBM— backing it.

Even if Swift is only ever used for Apple products, its impact could be bigger than any other programming language that has been created in recent years. With so many iPhones, iPads, and Macs in the hands of consumers, Swift will continue to be in high demand—and the opportunities for people who know how to program using it will be tremendous.

GLOSSARY

ANDROID A Linux-based mobile phone operating system developed by Google that powers smartphones, watches, tablets, and other devices.

APP Short for "application," an app is a set of written instructions for a computer to follow.

ARTIFICIAL INTELLIGENCE The ability of computer systems to perform tasks that normally require human intelligence; some examples include speech recognition, decision making, and visual perception.

BACK END The parts of a project that do the work that the user cannot see.

CLOUD A service that makes computer software and hardware available to users over the Internet.

CODE A language that tells technology what to do, or the act of writing instructions for technology using a programming language.

COMPILER A program that converts instructions into a form that can be read and executed by a computer.

DEEP LEARNING A machine learning technique whereby a machine learns tasks directly from data.

FRONT END The parts of a project that the user will interact with.

GITHUB A web-based hosting service where coding projects can be stored.

GRAPHICAL USER INTERFACE (GUI) Part of a program that consists of pictures, text boxes, buttons, or other graphics.

OBJECTIVE-C The primary programming language that was used to develop software for Apple products before Swift was released.

ONBOARDING PROCESS The application process that employees go through to work with a company such as Lyft.

OPEN SOURCE Denoting source code that is open, or available to anyone, and can be modified, changed, or redistributed.

PROGRAMMING The process of writing computer programs.

SERVER A computer designed to process requests and deliver data to another computer over the Internet or over a local network.

SERVER SIDE Operations that are performed by the server in a computer network.

SIMULATOR A part of Xcode that allows users to see how their code will run on any type of Apple device.

SOFTWARE DEVELOPMENT KIT (SDK) A collection of prebuilt programming libraries that helps users write apps quickly (libraries are collections of software that users can use when programming).

SWIFT A programming language created by Apple and released in 2014.

SYNTAX The set of rules, principles, and processes that govern the structure of a programming language.

XCODE A code editor that was developed by Apple that allows users to write code using the Swift programming language.

ACT/The App Association
1401 K Street NW, Suite 501
Washington, DC 20005
(202) 331-2130
Website: http://actonline.org
Facebook and Twitter: @actonline
Instagram: @act_online
This group of app companies and information technology firms
    focuses on mobile app development. They provide resources
    to help members promote their products, raise money,
    create jobs, and continue creating.

Association of Information Technology Professionals
3500 Lacey Road, Suite 100
Downers Grove, IL 60515
(630) 678-8300
Website: https://www.aitp.org
Facebook: @CompTIAAITP
Twitter: @CompTIA
This organization is dedicated to helping professionals,
    educators, and students expand their knowledge of
    technology and the industry as well as connect with
    their peers.

Association for Women in Computing (AWC)
PO Box 2768
Oakland, CA 94602
Website: http://www.awc-hq.org/home.html

This professional organization is focused on promoting the advancement of women in computer-related professions.

Code.org
1501 Fourth Avenue, Suite 900
Seattle, WA 98101
Facebook: @Code.org
Instagram and Twitter: @codeorg
This group is focused on increasing school participation in computer science education by making it available in every school.

IAENG Society of Software Engineering
Department of Computer Science Applied Statistics
University of New Brunswick
Saint John, NB E2L 4L5
Canada
Website: http://www.iaeng.org/ISSE.html
This organization is designed for engineers and scholars in the software engineering industry. The group's goal is to allow members to network, share information, exchange ideas, and solve problems impacting the software engineering community.

IEEE Computer Society
2001 L Street NW, Suite 700
Washington, DC 20036-4928
(202) 371-0101
Website: https://www.computer.org
Facebook: @ieeecomputersociety

Twitter: @ComputerSociety
This membership organization is dedicated to computer science and technology.

National Association of Programmers
PO Box 529
Prairieville, LA 70769
Website: http://www.napusa.org
This association is designed for programmers, developers, consultants, other professionals, and students in the computer industry. The overall goal of the group is to provide information and resources that give members a competitive edge in the ever-changing computer industry.

Scratch
MIT
75 Amherst Street
Cambridge, MA 02139
(617) 253-5960
Website: https://scratch.mit.edu/about
Facebook: @scratchteam
Instagram: @mitscratchteam
Twitter: @scratch
This free online resource allows people to program their own interactive stories, games, and animations and share those creations with others in an online community. It is a project of the Lifelong Kindergarten Group at the MIT Media Lab.

Women in Technology
200 Little Falls Street, Suite 205
Falls Church, VA 22046
(703) 349-1044
Website: http://www.womenintechnology.org
Facebook: @WITWomenDC
Twitter: @WITWomen
Based in the capital of the United States, this organization
    connects women who work in technology with one another
    through a mentoring program.

FOR FURTHER READING

Harmon, Daniel. *Powering Up a Career in Software Development and Programming*. New York, NY: Rosen Publishing, 2016.

Harris, Chris, and Patricia Harris. *Teaching Programming Concepts Through Play*. New York, NY: Rosen Publishing, 2015.

Heitkamp, Kristina Lyn. *Getting Paid to Make Games and Apps*. New York, NY: Rosen Publishing, 2017.

La Bella, Laura. *Building Apps*. New York, NY: Rosen Publishing, 2014.

McCue, Camille. *Coding for Kids for Dummies*. New York, NY: For Dummies, 2014.

Porterfield, Jason. *A Career as a Mobile App Developer*. New York, NY: Rosen Publishing, 2018.

Staley, Erin. *Career Building Through Creating Mobile Apps*. New York, NY: Rosen Publishing, 2014.

Sutherland, Adam. *The Story of Apple*. New York, NY: Rosen Publishing, 2012.

Wainewright, Max. *How to Code: A Step-by-Step Guide to Computer Coding*. New York, NY: Sterling Children's Books, 2016.

Winquist, Gloria, and Matt McCarthy. *Coding iPhone Apps for Kids: A Playful Introduction to Swift*. San Francisco, CA: No Starch Press, 2017.

Altexsoft. "The Good and the Bad of Swift Programming Language." June 14, 2017. https://www.altexsoft.com/blog /engineering/the-good-and-the-bad-of-swift-programming -language.

Apple, Inc. "Swift." Retrieved January 28, 2018. https://swift .org/about.

Apple Inc. "Swift. A Powerful Open Language That Lets Everyone Build Amazing Apps." Retrieved January 28, 2018. https://www.apple.com/swift.

Application Development Solutions Review. "Is Swift the Future of Server-Side Development?" September 12, 2017. https://solutionsreview.com/application-development /is-swift-the-future-of-server-side-development.

Bailey, Jeff. Developer of Intervals training app. Interview with the author. Columbus, Ohio, February 2018.

Chapman, Hamilton. "5 Reasons You Should Learn Swift in 2016." Pusher Blog, January 20, 2016. https://blog .pusher.com/5-reasons-you-should-learn-swift-in-2016-2.

Code.org. "Nine Policy Ideas to Make Computer Science Fundamental to K-12 Education." Retrieved March 26, 2018. https://code.org/files/Making_CS_Fundamental.pdf.

Code.org. "Promote Computer Science." Retrieved March 26, 2018. https://code.org/promote.

Empson, Rip. "Bustin Jieber: The 12-Year-Old App Developer Who Taught Himself to Code Goes Viral." TechCrunch, November 17, 2011. https://techcrunch.com/2011/11/17 /bustin-jieber-the-12-year-old-app-developer-who-taught -himself-to-code-goes-viral-video.

Etherington, Darrell. "Swift Creator Chris Lattner Joins Google Brain After Tesla Autopilot Stint." TechCrunch, August 14, 2017. https://techcrunch.com/2017/08/14 /swift-creator-chris-lattner-joins-google-brain-after-tesla -autopilot-stint.

Evans, Jonny. "Google Puts a Little of Apple's Swift in Its Future OS." Computerworld, November 24, 2017. https:// www.computerworld.com/article/3238042/apple-ios/google -puts-a-little-of-apple-s-swift-in-its-future-os.html.

Evans, Jonny. "12 Reasons to Learn Apple's Open-Source Swift Language." Computerworld, August 25, 2017. https://www .computerworld.com/article/3219732/apple-ios/12-reasons -to-learn-apples-open-source-swift-language.html.

Griffin, Andrew. "Apple's Developer Academy: Inside the Elite School Where iPhone Developers of the Future Are Being Trained." Independent, May 17, 2017. http://www .independent.co.uk/life-style/gadgets-and-tech /features/apple-developer-academy-iphone-developer -naples-school-training-elite-future-university -a7740546.html.

Lattner, Chris. "Chris Lattner's Homepage." Retrieved March 26, 2018. http://www.nondot.org/sabre.

Lattner, Chris. "Interview of Chris Lattner." Accidental Tech Podcast, January 17, 2017. http://atp.fm/205-chris-lattner -interview-transcript.

Metz, Cade. "Why Apple's Swift Language Will Instantly Remake Computer Programming." Wired, July 14, 2014. https://www.wired.com/2014/07/apple-swift.

Open Technology Institute. "Software's Impact and the Drive for Talent." New America, June 15, 2016. https://www

.newamerica.org/oti/events/softwares-economic-impact
-drive-talent.

Popper, Ben. "The Swift Effect: Apple's New Programming
Language Means Way More iPhone Developers and Apps."
Verge, June 2, 2014. https://www.theverge.com/apple
/2014/6/2/5773928/apple-swift-programming
-developers-objective-c.

Power, Jim, Executive Director, MedData. Interview with the
author. Columbus, Ohio, February 2018.

Rayome, Alison DeNisco. "The 10 Hottest Developer Jobs of
2017." TechRepublic, February 16, 2017. https://www
.techrepublic.com/article/the-10-hottest-developer-jobs
-of-2017.

Rubens, Paul. "10 Things You Should Know About Apple's
Swift." *CIO*, July 21, 2014. https://www.cio.com
/article/2456100/mobile-development/10-things
-you-should-know-about-apples-swift.html.

Solt, Paul. "Swift vs. Objective-C: 10 Reasons the Future
Favors Swift." *InfoWorld*, May 11, 2015. https://www
.infoworld.com/article/2920333/mobile-development/swift
-vs-objective-c-10-reasons-the-future-favors-swift.html.

Statt, Nick. "1 Billion Apple Devices Are in Active Use Around
the World." Verge, January 26, 2016. https://www.theverge
.com/2016/1/26/10835748/apple-devices-active-1-billion
-iphone-ipad-ios.

Suarez, Thomas. "Tom the Carrot." Retrieved March 26, 2018.
http://tomthecarrot.com.

Suarez, Thomas. "A 12-Year-Old App Developer." TEDx
Manhattan Beach, October 2011. https://www.ted.com/talks
/thomas_suarez_a_12_year_old_app_developer/transcript.

Tofel, Kevin. "After Apple Open Sources It, IBM Puts Swift Programming in the Cloud." ZDNet, December 4, 2015. http://www.zdnet.com/article/after-apple-open-sources -it-ibm-puts-swift-in-the-cloud.

"Toibe Index for January 2018." Retrieved January 28, 2018. https://www.tiobe.com/tiobe-index.

Tung, Liam. "Want a Developer Job? Time to Learn Apple's Swift as Demand Skyrockets." ZDNet, March 1, 2016. http://www.zdnet.com/article/want-a-developer-job -time-to-learn-apples-swift-as-demand-skyrockets.

INDEX

ABOUT THE AUTHOR

Sherri Mabry Gordon has authored multiple nonfiction books. Many of her books deal with issues teens face today, including everything from staying safe online to dealing with online trolls, public shaming, cyberbullying, and more. Gordon also writes about bullying for Verywell Family and has given multiple presentations to schools, churches, and the YMCA on bullying prevention, dating abuse, and online safety. She also volunteers regularly in her community's schools and serves on the school counselor advisory board for two schools. Gordon is passionate about seeing teens learn more about technology, especially how it can be used in beneficial ways. Gordon resides in Columbus, Ohio, with her husband, two children, and dog, Abbey.

PHOTO CREDITS

Cover, p. 23 Hero Images/Getty Images; cover, back cover, pp. 1, 4–5 (background) © iStockphoto.com/letoakin; p. 5 Rodin Eckenroth /FilmMagic/Getty Images; p. 8 Kyodo News/Getty Images; p. 10 Tal Revivo/Alamy Stock Vector; pp. 12, 34 Bloomberg/Getty Images; p. 16 photovibes/Shutterstock.com; p. 19 ESB Professional /Shutterstock.com; p. 26 Denys Prykhodov/Shutterstock.com; pp. 29 (top and bottom), 32 Siyavush Saidian; p. 36 Monkey Business Images/Shutterstock.com; p. 39 PSL Images/Alamy Stock Photo; p. 41 JuliusKielaitis/Shutterstock.com; p. 43 rvlsoft /Shutterstock.com; p. 45 Casimiro PT/Shutterstock.com; p. 48 Songquan Deng/Shutterstock.com.

Design and Layout: Nicole Russo-Duca; Editor: Siyavush Saidian; Photo Researcher: Karen Huang